CW01654834

Chris Culshaw and David Craig

Oxford University Press

Acknowledgements

The publishers would like to thank the following for permission to reproduce photographs:

Boots Company PLC - Baby Business Centre: p.18 (both);

John Walmsley: p.7 (both), 8, 14 (both), 55 (all), 60, 62.

The illustrations are by Katherine Baxter, Phillip Burrows, Elitta Fell, Debbie Hinks, Alan Marks, Mike Nicholson, Viv Quillin and Ursula Sieger.

The cover illustration is by Jason Pizzey.

Oxford University Press, Walton Street, Oxford OX2 6DP

Oxford New York Toronto
Delhi Bombay Calcutta Madras Karachi
Petaling Jaya Singapore Hong Kong Tokyo
Nairobi Dar es Salaam Cape Town
Melbourne Auckland

and associated companies in
Berlin Ibadan

Oxford is a trade mark of Oxford University Press

ISBN 019 833389 7

Typeset by Tradespools Ltd, Frome, Somerset
Printed in Great Britain by Scotprint Ltd, Musselburgh

Contents

Friday the Thirteenth

Louise woke up with a start and looked at her alarm clock. It was 8.22 am. She should have been up and out of the house by 8.15. She picked up the clock and shook it. Then she saw that she had set it to go off at nine o'clock, instead of seven.

She got washed, dressed and left the house at exactly 8.45. If she ran all the way, she might just catch the 8.50 bus at the corner. She was only a few yards from home when it started to rain very hard. She had forgotten her umbrella, so she ran back to the house to get it. She looked at her watch. It was now 8.48. She might still catch the bus if she hurried. But she got to the corner just as the bus pulled away from the stop, at 8.51 am.

Mrs Stone got up, as usual, at 7.30 am. She had a shower, dressed and made breakfast. She listened to the 8 o'clock news on the radio, before doing her yoga exercises. At 8.45 she put on her coat and took her dog for his morning walk.

As she was crossing the road near the bus stop she tripped and fell. The narrow heel of her right shoe was stuck in a grid. As Mrs Stone struggled to get it free she let go of the dog's lead.

The dog ran into the road.

Simon Black got up at 8.15 am. He had overslept because he had been to a party the night before. He had a hangover so he didn't feel like any breakfast. He went to get his car from the garage, but it wouldn't start. He decided to walk to work, but just as he left the house, at 8.45, it started to rain. Simon went back into the garage and tried once more to start the car. This time it started.

He backed out into the street and drove up the road towards the bus stop. By now it was raining hard. His windscreen was misted over. Simon turned on the heater to clear it.

It was at that exact moment that Simon Black saw the dog run out in front of his car. He braked as hard as he could but the road was very wet. His car skidded right across the road, onto the pavement. It hit Louise, who was standing at the bus stop. She was rushed to hospital with a broken leg.

What to do

Copy the diagram on page 3 and label it clearly to show how the accident happened.

What to do next

Make a list of all the events that played a part in Louise's accident.
Write your answer like this:

1 Louise set her alarm clock wrongly.
2 .....

Good Luck, Bad Luck

Some people believe that superstitions like those mentioned here are true. They believe that good and bad luck play a big part in all our lives. They never walk under ladders. If they spill some salt they always throw a pinch over their shoulder. Other people think superstitions like these are nonsense. They claim such sayings have been passed down from the 'dark ages', when people believed in demons, fairies and witchcraft.

1 If your cat sneezes three times, you will have bad luck.

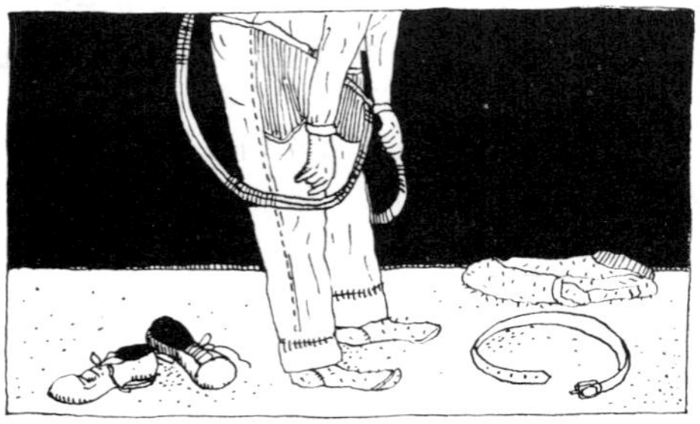

2 If you accidentally put your trousers on inside out, you will have good luck.

3 If you have long fingers, you will never make money.

4 If you meet a black cat on your way to a football match, your team will lose.

5 If you tread on a grave, you will have bad luck.

6 If your right hand itches, you will get some money. If your left hand itches, you will be giving some away.

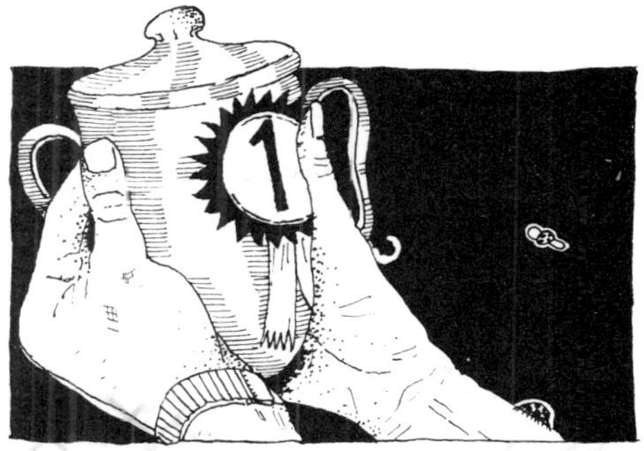

7 If a ladybird lands on your arm, you will have good luck.

8 Never refuse a mince pie or you will have ten years' bad luck.

9 If a money spider runs over your foot, you will soon be able to afford some new clothes.

10 Never invite thirteen friends to a party or you or one of your friends will have bad luck.

What to do

Oral work in pairs or in small groups

1 Do you believe in any of these superstitions?

2 Do you know of any other superstitions?

3 Do you think people are more or less superstitious nowadays than they were a hundred years ago?

4 Do you think men are more superstitious than women?

A Thousand Broken Legs

Lisa is a very superstitious person. Her friend, Sonya, thinks superstitions are 'a load of claptrap'.

Lisa: Last week my dad walked under a ladder and ten minutes later he fell over and broke his leg.
Sonya: So what?
Lisa: That proves I'm right. Superstitions aren't 'a load of claptrap'.
Sonya: Just because two things happen at the same time doesn't mean they're connected, idiot!
Lisa: What do you mean?
Sonya: Your dad's a painter. He must have walked under a thousand ladders. But he hasn't had a thousand broken legs, has he?
Lisa: Of course he hasn't!
Sonya: That proves it's all claptrap, doesn't it?
Lisa: It doesn't prove anything!

The next day Lisa did an experiment to try to prove she was right.

Lisa borrowed a ladder and put it up against the side of a shop. She wrote down how many people walked under the ladder and how many people walked round it. In one hour 164 people walked by the shop and 144 of these walked round the ladder. Only 20 walked under it.

Lisa told Sonya about her experiment and said, 'My experiment proves it is bad luck to walk under ladders. If it isn't bad luck why did so many people walk round the ladder?'

What to do

1 Sonya was not convinced by Lisa's experiment. What do you think she said to Lisa?

2 Sonya decided to do her own experiment to see if the superstition about ladders and luck was true. Describe an experiment she might have set up.

Same Time, Same Place

Kate and Santi were born in the same maternity hospital, at the same time, on the same day.

Kate
Kate weighed only 2.50 kg when she was born. She had problems breathing and had to be given oxygen.

Her mother went to antenatal clinic regularly and read a lot about baby care. Kate was breast fed and soon put on weight. Kate's parents lived in a tiny rented cottage in a small village. The cottage had a big garden. Kate's mother grew a lot of fruit and vegetables. Kate's father was an unemployed farm-worker. Both sets of grandparents lived nearby. Kate had no brothers or sisters. Kate's parents did not own a car.

Santi
Santi weighed 4 kg at birth. Santi's mother wanted to breast feed her baby but could not. Santi's mother was not married. She was a teacher. She had been living with Santi's father (a long distance lorry driver) for seven years. Santi had one brother, Godwin, who was eighteen months old when Santi was born.

Santi's parents lived in a small flat, near the centre of a large town. They had no garden, but there was a park nearby. There was a large industrial estate near the flat. Santi's mother's parents lived in Jamaica. Santi's mother owned a car.

What to do

Writing

1 What might have helped to give Kate a good start in life?

2 What might have had the opposite effect?

3 What might have helped to give Santi a good start in life?

4 What might have had the opposite effect?

5 Answer the same two questions about your own start in life. You may have to ask your parents about your very early childhood and their life-style before you were born.

6 Which of the two babies had the best start in life?

Sarah and Alison Gower are identical twins. They are 4 years old.

What to do

Oral work in pairs or in small groups

1 In what ways would you expect Sarah and Alison to be the same when they are 14 years old? In what ways would you expect them to be different?

2 If genetic engineers could produce a person who was identical to you in every way, how do you think you would feel on meeting your 'double' for the first time?

3 If your double did exist what kinds of problems might this cause?

4 Why might it be useful to have such a double?

Just a Matter of Luck?

It's just a matter of luck where and when we are born, whether we are an only child or born into a large family, whether our parents are in or out of work.

It is not easy to decide how important these things might be. They may influence our life chances in a number of ways.

What to do

Copy the table below and complete it.
Give each of the factors a rating from 0 to 10. (Rating a factor 0 means it will not effect our life chances at all, and rating a factor at 10 means it will have a very big effect on our life chances.)

← Copy this part only →

Factors		**Rating (0–10)**
1 Your parents' jobs	**1**	
2 The size of your family when you were born	**2**	
3 The size of the house you lived in	**3**	
4 The area/district you were born in	**4**	
5 Your weight at birth	**5**	
6 Your parent's health/fitness	**6**	
7 Your skin colour	**7**	
8 Your mother's age	**8**	
9 Your father's age	**9**	
10	**10**	
11	**11**	
12	**12**	

Think of three more factors to add to the list and give each one a rating.

What to do next

Compare your ratings for the factors listed on page 9 with others in your class or group. Find out which factors were rated highly by the class or group. Copy and complete these sentences:

1 The most highly rated factors were ...

2 I think these factors might have an important effect on a person's life chances because ...

If only

When I was 14 my dad was ill and had to give up work. He wanted to live by the sea, so we bought a house in Brighton. I had to leave all my friends and go to a new school.

It was the worst year of my life. All the people in my class had friends and didn't want me butting in. The only people who would go around with me were a couple of thugs called Bradley and Turner. I hated them, but went around with them because I was so desperate for friends. They used to do stupid things like smashing windows in bus shelters. I did the same stupid things too, just to keep in with them.

I liked school and was good at quite a few things. If I worked hard and got good marks Bradley and Turner used to call me a swot. So I stopped trying.

If only my dad hadn't been ill. If only he hadn't wanted to retire to Brighton. If only ...

What to do

Think of an 'if only' event that has changed the course of your life. Write a few sentences about this event. Describe what might have happened in your life if this event had not happened.

Just Like a Game of Cards?

Life is just like a game of cards. If you are born with a good hand, you will be one of life's winners.

We don't have any say in how our lives will work out. It's up to God. God has plans for us all, and nothing we do can change that.

Nobody has the foggiest idea how their life is going to turn out. It's just pure chance, like tossing a dice. One day you could be on top of the world, the next day you could be down and out.

If you've got money, you can have the sort of life that poor people can only dream about. If you've got money, you can do anything with your life.

It's rubbish to say that life is a gamble, that depends on chance! If you put your mind to it you can do anything you like. If things don't work out then we've only ourselves to blame.

What to do

Oral work in pairs or in small groups

1 Say if you agree or disagree with the five statements given above.

2 What kinds of thing might play a part in shaping the pattern of your life?

Life Chances Abroad

All babies are born equal . . . but some are born more equal than others.

	Country A	Country B
Population	3.4 million	2.8 million
Life expectancy	49 years	64 years
Infant mortality (number of deaths per 1000 live births)	62	114
Number of nurses per 1000 population	2	1
Income per household per year	£420	£700
Percentage population who can read/write	70% males 65% females	46% males 10% females
Length of schooling	7 years	4 years
Percentage of girls educated	90%	10%
Percentage of population with access to clean water	70%	50%
Percentage of population able to vote	60% (adult males only)	100%
Percentage country's income spent on arms	11%	8%
Exports	Timber, Cocoa, rice	Cotton, sugar

What to do

Writing

Answer these questions, using the information in the table opposite. Give reasons for your answers.

1 Which country has the healthiest population, A or B?
2 Which country has the best educated work-force?
3 If you were an adult female which country would you choose to live in, A or B?
4 If you were an adult male which would you choose?
5 What is the biggest difference between countries A and B and your own country?
6 Both countries spend about one-tenth of their wealth on weapons. How do you think this might affect the life chances of their citizens?
7 Could A be a country in Europe?
8 Could B be a country in Asia?
9 If you were going to start up your own business in one of these countries, which would you choose?
10 What additional facts should be added to the table opposite to give a more accurate picture of A and B?

What to do next

Role play and writing

1 The governments of countries A and B are asking the United Nations for financial help to overcome their problems. The United Nations has £10 million to share between the two countries.

2 Role play meetings between officials from the United Nations and officials from countries A and B.
At these meetings the officials from countries A and B have to say how they would spend the UN money to improve the life chances of children and adults in their country.

3 Imagine you are a government official of country A or B.
Twenty years have passed since your country was given money by the UN to help to improve the life chances of your people. The UN has asked you to write a short report on the changes in your country over the last twenty years.

When is Enough Enough?

Marion
Do you know what's wrong with kids these days? They don't know the real value of money. Last week a boy at our school paid £100 for a pair of trainers. That's immoral: £100 would feed a third-world family for a year. I don't know how he could do it. I wouldn't feel comfortable wearing them. But we are under a lot of pressure to spend, spend, spend.

Some kids I know fill their rooms with consumer junk, like squirrels storing nuts for the winter. We are the target of a lot of clever advertising by very powerful companies. They think all young people are hooked on things. These admen see us as junkies who are hooked on records and clothes and the latest electronic toys. I wear my clothes until they wear out. I buy what I need, not what I'm conned into buying.

And every useless bit of consumer junk uses up more of the Earth's resources. We are killing the planet because we are too stupid to say 'No!' when the admen say 'Spend, spend, spend!'

Scott
I like good gear. There's nothing wrong with looking smart. Some of these kids who get their clothes from Oxfam shops and jumble sales make me sick. They go around like tramps and have the cheek to say *we* are antisocial!

You've got to have style. You've got to have the latest records. If you don't, then you don't fit in, you don't belong. You'd find it hard to make friends. You can't go to a disco in second-hand cast-offs. It helps your self-confidence if you're dressed to kill in the latest gear. People notice you.

Everyone wants to own things, it's only natural. These freaks who say that having possessions is bad are stupid. They all sleep in beds, don't they? They all eat at tables, use knives and forks, drink from cups. So they own dozens of things. They are just hypocrites who want to drag everyone down to their level. Besides, when I buy a new pair of jeans I am helping the people who work in the jeans factory to have a better life. If I didn't buy those jeans they wouldn't have a job.

What to do

Oral work in pairs or in small groups
Answer these questions. Give reasons for your answers.

1 Is it 'immoral' to pay £100 for a pair of trainers?
2 Are young people really 'hooked on things'?
3 What does Marion mean when she says, 'We're killing the planet'?
4 Is it 'natural' to want to own things?
5 Why does Scott think people like Marion are 'hypocrites'?
6 Choose one of the arguments and say why you agree or disagree with it.

What to do next

Imagine that you are very rich. You would like to leave a part of your vast fortune to some individuals or small groups who will use it for unusual projects.

Find out how you would go about writing a will and think of the groups you would leave your wealth to. Then write your own will.

Testing a Product

The manager of a local clothing factory wants your class or group to test a new range of jeans her company is planning to market next spring. She has given you 30 pairs of the new jeans in various sizes and colours. She has offered a prize of £100 to anyone who can think of a good brand name for the jeans.

She has also offered to pay £500 to anyone who can think of a very unusual idea for a TV commercial to promote the jeans.

She wants your group to prepare a detailed report after they have tested the jeans for one month. She also wants permission to use any part of the report in her advertising campaign.

What to do

1 List all the qualities of the jeans that you would want to investigate. e.g. Will they fade when washed?

2 Describe how the jeans should be tested, so that the factory manager will be given the maximum information at the end of the month's trial.

3 The information each 'tester' gathers has to be recorded on a printed form. Design a form for this purpose using the information you have put together on how the jeans will be tested.

4 Invent some brand names for the jeans.

5 Outline in two or three sentences an idea for a TV commercial to promote the jeans.

What to do next

When the jeans went on the market, the following claims appeared in the advertisements for them.

> **Tough jeans for tough kids!**
>
> We asked some tough school kids to test our new jeans for us and they told us they are the best jeans in the world. They wore them for a month, day and night, and tried their best to destroy them. But they couldn't. Nothing can touch them. They are built to last for ever.
>
> Our tough guys and gals washed our jeans hundreds of times and they never faded. The zips will never break and all the seams are double-stitched in unbreakable thread.
>
> Our tough testers all liked the jeans because they made them look good.
>
> **And when you look good, you feel good!**

Your group made a truthful report, which included good and bad points about the jeans. When they read this advertisement they were upset because it did not give an accurate picture of the report they wrote on the jeans.

Which parts of the advertisement do you think your group would find unacceptable? Write your answers like this:

1 They told us they were the best jeans in the world. The group would not have said this because they would have had to test thousands of pairs of jeans to prove this was true.

Baby Buggies

You have been asked to test five folding baby buggies. The results of your investigation are shown in the table below:

	Buggy				
Feature	**A**	**B**	**C**	**D**	**E**
1 Is it strong?	√		√	√	√
2 Is it light?	√	√	√		√
3 Does it fold up small?	√	√			
4 Does it give a smooth ride?	√		√		√
5 Does it have safety straps?		√		√	√
6 Is it bright/colourful?			√		
7 Is it hard to tip over?				√	√
8 Does it have good brakes?		√		√	
9 Is the seat comfortable?	√	√	√		
10 Is the price reasonable?	√		√	√	√

What to do

1 Which buggy do you think is the 'best buy'? Give reasons for your choice.

2 You have been asked to test six personal stereos and decide on one as the best buy. Make a list of 10 features you would evaluate. List them in rank order, putting the most important feature first.

— Consumer Law and Consumer Rights —

There are many laws governing the buying and selling of goods, but the main law affecting young people is the Sale of Goods Act 1979.

The Sale of Goods Act 1979 states that:

1 The goods you buy must be 'as described'.
e.g. A 100 per cent wool sweater must be just that.

2 The goods must be of 'merchantable quality'.
i.e. they must not be broken, they must work properly, etc.

3 The goods must be 'fit for the purpose'.
e.g. An item sold as a tin-opener must be capable of opening tins.

Consumer law is quite complicated, but you can get free advice and leaflets about it from your local Trading Standards Officer/Consumer Protection Officer or the Office of Fair Trading.

Here are some of the questions that young people often ask at the Trading Standards Office:

Q: Is it legal for a shop to put up a sign saying 'No refunds given' or 'No articles can be returned?'

A: No, this is illegal. Any shop doing this should be reported to your TSO right away.

Q: I saw some goods in a shop window and went into the shop to buy them. The shopkeeper would not sell me the item out of the window, but insisted I had the same item from under the counter. Were they right to do this?
A: The shopkeeper has the right to refuse to sell you anything.

Q: If I return some faulty goods to a shop after a few weeks, am I still covered by the Act?
A: The Act says you must not keep the goods for more than a 'reasonable' length of time before returning them. But the Act does not say precisely how long a 'reasonable' length of time is.

Q: Do I have to produce a receipt when I return faulty goods?
A: The Act does *not* say you must have a receipt. But if you can produce a receipt you will be more likely to get a refund.

Q: If I return some faulty item to a shop and the shopkeeper says, 'Don't complain to me! Write to the makers,' what should I say?
A: Tell the shopkeeper that they are in the wrong. The Act says very clearly that the retailer (the shopkeeper) is responsible, not the firm that made the goods.

Q: If I return a faulty pair of shoes and the shopkeeper tells me that they haven't got another pair like them, do I have to accept a credit note?
A: No, you do *not* have to accept a credit note. You are not entitled to have the original goods replaced but most good shops *do* offer to replace the original item. You are, however, entitled to a full cash refund. A credit note can only be spent in that store, and you may be dissatisfied with the service you have had there.

Q: I bought some goods and only discovered they had a fault when I got them home. When I took them back, the shopkeeper said they couldn't be replaced because I hadn't noticed the fault in the shop. Was this correct?
A: No, the goods are still covered by the Act and can be replaced. (Obviously the quicker you return the goods the better.)

Q: Is it illegal for a shop to display goods without price tags?
A: No, but food and drink in self-service shops must be priced.

Q: If I put a deposit on an item, like a bike, and then find out I can't afford it, can I get my deposit back?
A: No, and you may even be asked to pay more money to the shopkeeper if they have lost money because you have not bought the item!

What to do

Oral work in pairs or in small groups

1 Use the information opposite to decide who is on the right side of the law in the five situations below.

2 Have you ever had to tackle a problem like this? If so, did you feel you knew enough about your rights?

3 Do you know where to find your local Trading Standards Office?

A John went into a shop to look at some shirts. He saw one he liked but (like the others on the rack) it had no price tag. He took it to the till to ask how much it was. The manager said it was £25, quickly wrapped it up and then asked John for the money. John said he didn't want the shirt because it was too expensive. The manager got angry and pointed to a sign that said, 'No browsers. Genuine shoppers only.' The manager demanded payment. John said, 'I don't have to buy this shirt.'

Who was right?

B Denise took a faulty watch back to the shop. The manager was very helpful. She gave Denise the name and address of the company who made the watch, telling her to post the watch to them. Denise did not want to do this. She said the shop should put the matter right. The manager disagreed, saying, 'After all, I only sell these watches, I don't make them!'

Who was right?

C Steve took some faulty trainers back to the big supermarket where he had bought them three days before. The woman on the customer service desk asked Steve for his receipt. He did not have it. The woman said, 'Well, you can't expect a refund can you? How do we know you bought these trainers here? You can have bought them anywhere.' Steve disagreed.

Who was right?

D Jill returned a skirt to a shop because the label said it was 100 per cent cotton, but it was clearly made from a cheap man-made (acrylic) fibre. The manager said, 'This is a perfect skirt. It's your size and it's the colour you wanted. You can't expect us to change it.' Jill insisted that she did.

Who was right?

E Karla went to ask if she could exchange a swimsuit (she had bought the wrong size) and the manager just pointed to a notice above the till which said, 'No articles returned'. Karla said she would go to the Trading Standards Office because she was sure she should be able to change the swimsuit. The shopkeeper said she was wrong.

Who was right?

The Hamburger Connection

One Saturday morning a group of young people gathered outside a fast-food restaurant. They handed out leaflets to young customers as they entered and left.

After a while the manager came out and asked them politely, but firmly, to move. The group politely, but firmly, refused.

A policewoman appeared. She asked the group to move away from the doorway, saying they were causing an obstruction. The group moved away from the restaurant, but continued to hand out leaflets. The leaflets said:

Stop!

Before you eat at this restaurant you should know:

- This company buys millions of tonnes of beef every year from countries such as Brazil.
- To provide grazing land for the cattle millions of acres of tropical forest have been destroyed.
- These forests were home for people and animals. Both have been ruthlessly displaced by the bulldozer and the beef steer. These forests are the lungs of our planet.

Think!

What can you do?

1. Stop eating hamburgers made from beef.
2. Try alternative non-meat snacks.
3. Write to the company (address overleaf) and tell them why you won't be using their restaurants any more. You have real spending power. Money talks.
4. Write to one of the embassies (addresses overleaf) and make your protest about the destruction of the rain forests.

When a local radio station did a programme about the group they invited the manager of the restaurant to come into the studio to meet members of the group and debate the issue. This is how the discussion started:

Manager: Quite frankly, I think these young people are well-meaning fools. They are doing their best to put people out of work, not just in this town, where unemployment is at nearly 25 per cent, but in poor countries like Brazil.

Protester: That's a stupid argument.

Manager: If you were on the dole you wouldn't think it was stupid.

What to do

Writing

Continue the argument between the manager and the protester. Set it out as above and use the information given in the leaflet to help you.

What to do next

Answer these questions. Give reasons for your answers.

1 Why did the protesters hand out leaflets to young customers?

2 What does 'spending power' mean?

3 What sort of non-meat snacks could a fast-food restaurant serve?

4 Your favourite canned drink contains cane sugar. You discover that this sugar is processed in factories that employ child labourers. These children are paid terrible wages and they work in dangerous and unhealthy conditions. What would you do in response?

New Laws

Having a baby

What if: A new law was passed that said, 'In future couples will only be allowed to have *one* child'?

What to do

Writing

1 Why do you think such a law might be passed?

2 How do you think this law would affect the decisions of couples thinking about having a child?

3 What disadvantages does this law have for such couples?

4 On balance do you think this would be a good law? Give reasons for your answer.

Free to choose

What if: A new law was passed that said, 'Young people do NOT have to attend school if they don't want to'?

At present the law forces a young person to attend school for 6 hours a day, 200 days a year, for 10 years. If they do not attend they are breaking the law.

But this new law would mean that young people would be free to choose which school they went to and which lessons they attended.

What to do

Writing

1 List the advantages of this law for young people.

2 List its disadvantages for young people.

3 List the advantages of this law for teachers.

4 List its disadvantages for teachers.

5 On balance do you think this would be a good law? Give reasons for your answer.

6 If this law came into force, what would you do about your schooling?

Becoming an adult

What if: A new law was passed that said, 'To become an adult you have to pass a special exam'?

At present anyone over the age of 18 is considered to be an adult. This is clearly a very silly idea. Some people are very mature at 15 years of age, while others are still very immature at the age of 25. Under this law, only people who have passed the Adulthood Exam would be allowed to vote, drive a car, buy alcohol, etc. A person would be able to take the exam at any age.

What to do

Oral work in pairs or in small groups

1 Do you think this law is a good idea?

2 Do you think there would be problems enforcing it?

3 How old do you think most people in your group would be when they passed the Adulthood Exam?

4 What sort of adulthood skills do you think should be tested by the exam?

5 If adulthood skills were taught in schools and colleges, what sorts of people would be best qualified to teach them?

Two Heads are Better than One

What if: Human brains could be connected together like this?

Person A could experience what Person B experiences. They would share the same feelings and the same ideas.
Person A could also use the brain power of person B, or vice versa.
Or they could combine their brain power.

What to do

Writing

How would you answer the following questions? Write your answers down.

1 What would be the advantages of this invention?
2 What would be its disadvantages?
3 What sort of uses might it have?
4 What might happen if the following connections were made?

Identical twins

A very young person

A very old person

A gentle person

An aggressive person

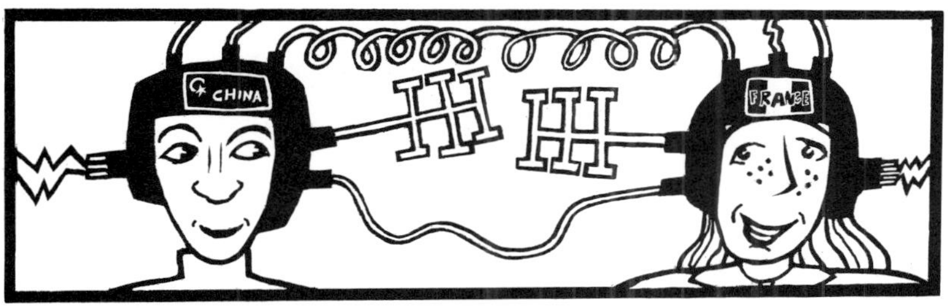

A Chinese person

A French person

5 What might happen if this kind of connection was tried?

6 What do you think would happen if all the human brains in the world were connected using this invention?

7 If it was possible to connect your brain with that of an animal, which animals would you choose to be linked with, and why?

States of Mind

What if: A drug was discovered that made anyone who took it feel very happy all the time. (This drug is cheap, easy to make and is non-addictive.)

What to do

Oral work in pairs or in small groups

1. What would be the advantages of using this drug?
2. What would be the disadvantages for the user?
3. On balance, would the drug be a good or a bad thing for society? Give reasons for your answer.
4. What difference would this drug make to your family?
5. What difference would it make to your school?

Anything is possible

What if: A whole range of safe, cheap drugs were discovered that changed human behaviour and human abilities in the following ways:

Drug A
Makes you good at Maths.

Drug B
Makes you think a thousand times faster than normal.

Drug C
Makes you handsome or beautiful.

Drug D
Makes you see into the future.

Drug E
Makes you super-strong.

Drug F
Makes you see into the past.

Drug G
Makes you fly like a bird.

Drug H
Makes you weightless.

Drug I
Makes you wise.

Drug K
Makes you musical.

What to do

Oral work in pairs or in small groups

1 If you could try one of these drugs, which would you choose and why?

2 Which of these drugs would have the most disruptive effect if it was used by young people? Give reasons for your answer.

3 Which drug would have the biggest effect on family life? Give reasons for your answer.

4 If you take two of the drugs at the same time you experience both effects. e.g. If you take drugs G and K together you become a musical bird. Which two drugs would you combine and why?

5 If you could invent a new drug, what effect would you like it to have and why?

Work, Work, Work!

What if: A law was passed that said, 'Nobody must be without a job. Any person without a job will be twinned with a person in work. They will share the job and the wages'?

What to do

Oral work in pairs/small groups

1 What advantages would this law have for you and your family?

2 What would the disadvantages of this law be for you and your family?

Pride in your work

What if: A law was passed that said, 'Nobody will make or sell cheap, sub-standard goods. If workers are asked to make or sell goods that they think are rubbish, they will report their company to the police'?

This law would put an end to toys that fall to pieces after five minutes. It would see the end of cheap, badly-fitting clothes that shrink or fade or fall apart after one wash.

What to do

Writing

1 What effect would this law have on companies who make and sell goods?

2 What effect would it have on the workers in these companies?

3 What effect would it have on you as a shopper and consumer?

4 What sort of things at present on sale in local shops might disappear?

5 On balance, would this be a good law? Give reasons for your answer.

What if: **A law was passed that said, 'In the future a person's wages will depend on how useful their job is to the community. People like sewage workers, who do vital work, will be highly paid. They will earn much more than pop stars or footballers who do not do useful work'?**

What to do

Oral work in pairs or in small groups

1 Which jobs would have higher pay if this law was passed?

2 Which jobs would have lower pay?

3 On balance do you think it would be a good or a bad law? Give reasons for your answer.

4 If this law was passed what effect would it have on your choice of job?

Pets Limited

What if: A new law was passed that said, 'Nobody is allowed to have a pet unless they can convince their local Pet Control Office that they have a good reason for having one'?

What to do

Oral work in pairs or in small groups

1 Why do you think a law like this might be passed?

2 What sort of people might have a good reason for having a pet?

3 Who would suffer because of this law?

4 Who would benefit from it?

Reincarnation Inc

What if: A scientist proved that when we die, we are born again (reincarnated) as an animal? This same scientist has also found a way of controlling what we are reincarnated as. She put the following advert in the paper.

Reincarnation Inc

Don't be a worm or a slug in your next life! We can make sure you will come back as cat or a dog, or even a horse.

The more you pay, the more lovable and intelligent you will be in your second life. Prices from £10 (you come back as an ant) up to £20,000 (you come back as a very smart dolphin!)

Write now for details. PO Box 707, Carnbridge Clarion, Carnbridge, CB1 2LJ

What to do

Writing

1 What animal would you like to be reincarnated as? Give reasons for your answer?

2 How would you like your worst enemy to be reincarnated?

3 What long-term effects would Reincarnation Inc have on human society?

4 What long-term effects would it have on the animal world?

5 Make up a price list for Reincarnation Inc's charges, starting from an ant at £10 and going up to dolphins at £20000. Include as many different animals as you can think of.

What to do next

Role play

You have died and come back to Earth as an animal of your choice. You have been asked to appear on a TV chat show to talk about what it's like to be reincarnated. Role play your discussion with someone else acting as the TV presenter. Then swap roles.

Life Span Ltd

What if: Somebody found a way of extending our life span, so we could all live until we were 600 years old? You could choose how you would age over these 600 years from three different options.
The three options are:

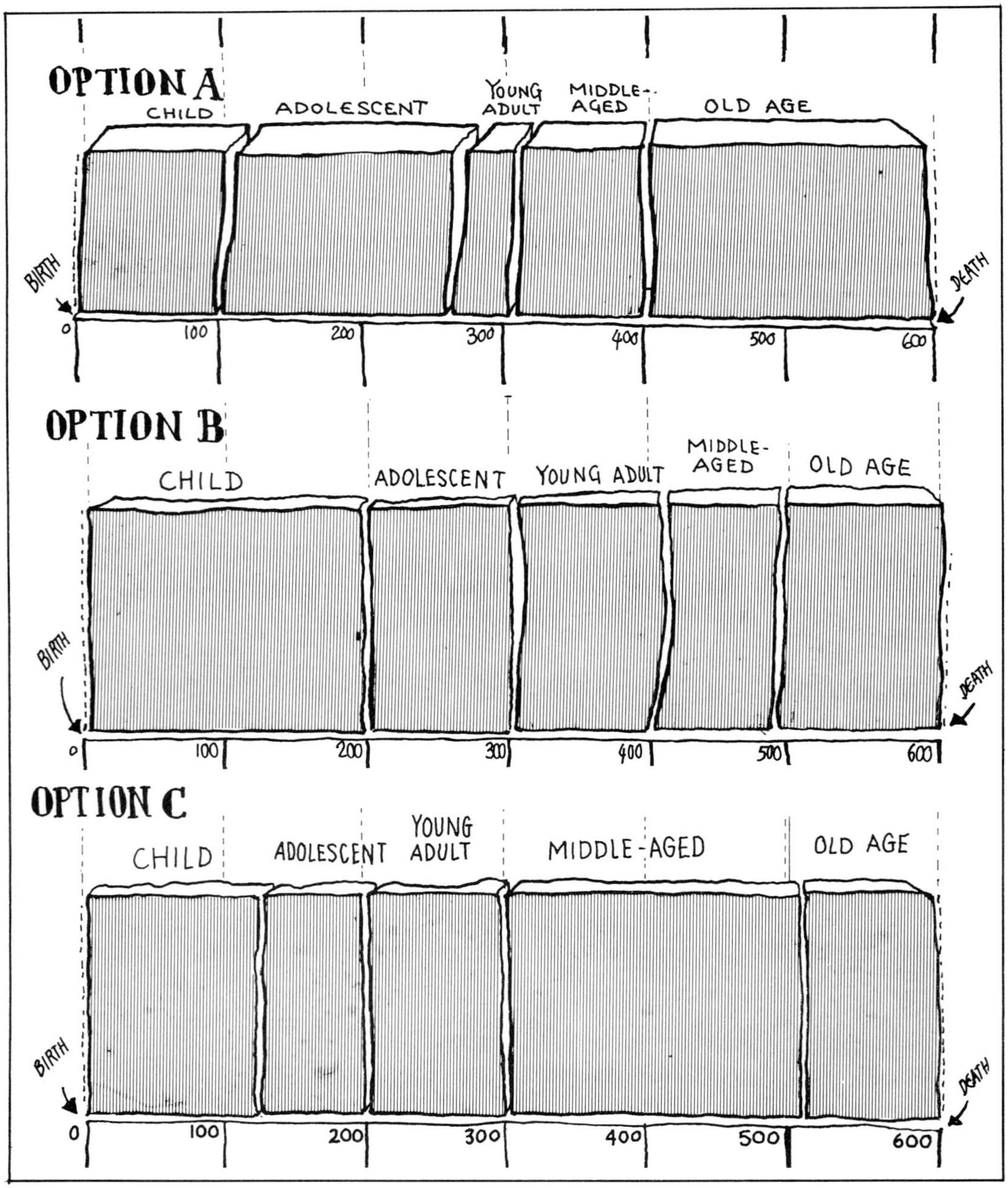

What to do

Writing

1 Which of the three options would you choose?
It may help you to answer this question if you make a table like the one below:

Option	Advantages	Disadvantages
A		
B		
C		

2 Why did you choose this option? What didn't you like about the others?

3 Which option would have the most beneficial effect on society? Why?

4 Which would have the most damaging effect? Why?

5 If you could design your own life pattern for a 600 year life-span, what would it be? Draw a lifeline like the ones opposite to show the pattern you would choose.

What if: A scientist invented a machine that took people back into the past?

What to do

Oral work in pairs or in small groups

1 What sort of problems would this machine create?

2 What sort of benefits might it have?

3 On balance do you think this machine would have good or bad effects in the long term?

4 If you could use this machine what period in history would you go back to? Give reasons for your answer.

Nepto

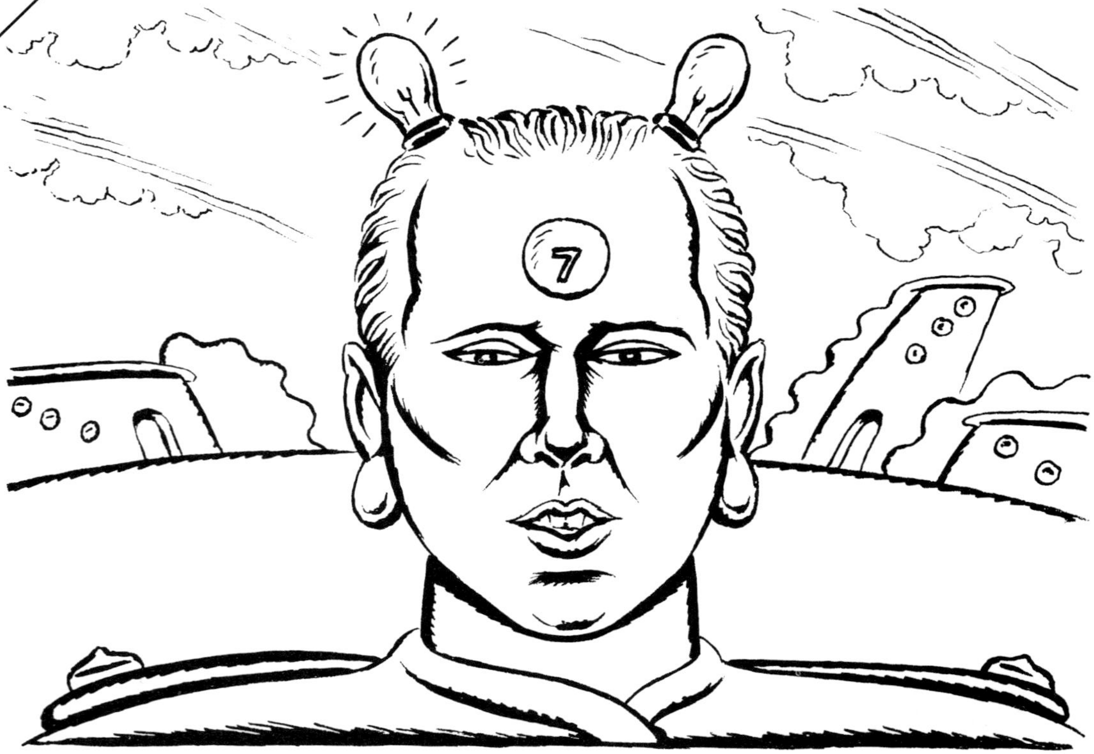

Last week a spaceship from Earth discovered a new planet, Nepto. The captain of the spaceship sent back this message about the people on Nepto.

'Neptonians look just like Earth people and we had very little trouble communicating with them. In many ways they behave just like people on Earth but in other ways they are very different. For example, all young people on Nepto, between the ages of 3 and 15, have two light bulbs fitted into the top of their heads. One light is red and the other is green. These young people also have a counter, rather like a digital watch, fitted to their forehead.

'When we asked about this we were told that on Nepto everyone is trained to tell the truth. As soon as a girl or boy is 3 years old they have the lights and the counter fitted to their skull. They have to wear these all day and every day until they are 15 years old.

'The bulbs light up whenever they speak. If they speak the truth the green light comes on. If they tell a lie, the red bulb lights up.

'The counter keeps a running total of all the lies each young person tells in a week. At the end of each week all youngsters have to go to their local Truth Centre. Here the Truth Officers record their weekly totals and reset everyone's counter to zero. That way everybody makes a fresh start each week.

'This graph shows how the average Neptonian youngster is trained to tell the truth:

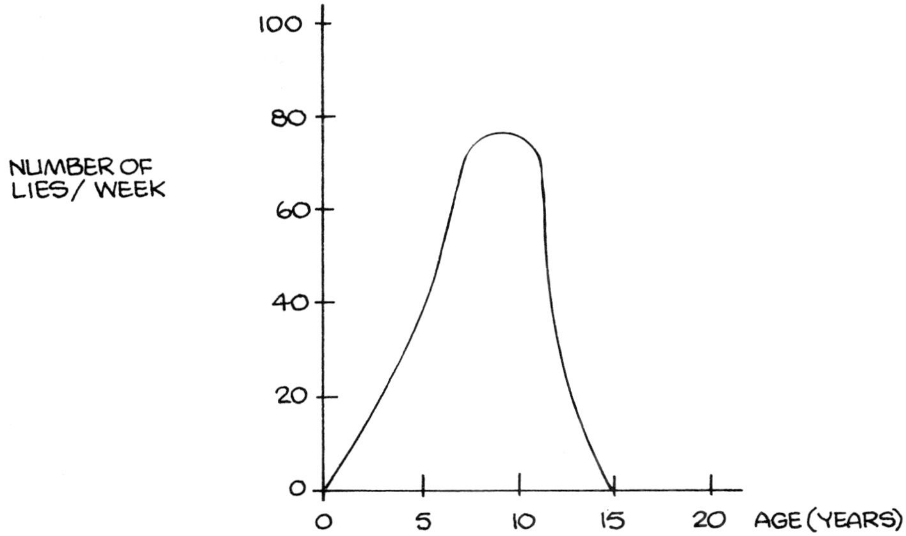

'By the time they are 15 years old most Neptonians have stopped telling lies. Then the light bulbs and counter are removed and then (and only then) are youngsters on Nepto allowed to marry, have children and vote.'

What to do

Oral work in pairs or in small groups

Answer these questions. Give reasons for your answers.

1 Why do you think the lights and counters are not fitted to Neptonians at birth?

2 How do the lights help to train the young Neptonians to speak the truth?

3 What conclusions can you draw from the graph?

4 If this system was used here on Earth, what good effects and what bad effects might it have?

Chained Story

Have you heard about Darren Hope's dad? He was caught shop-lifting again. He tried to steal a jacket. My mum reckons he'll go to jail this time.

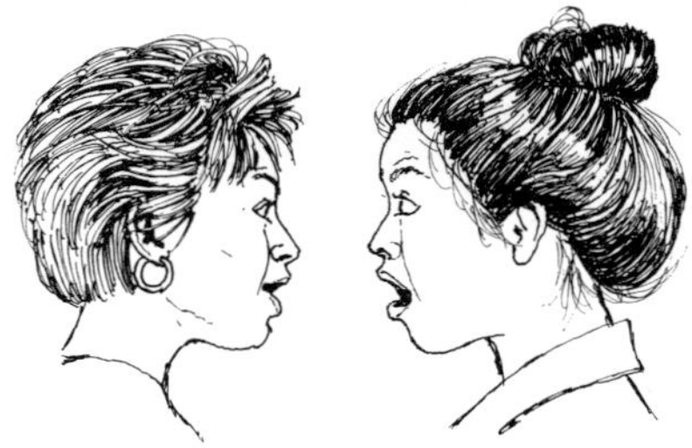

A → B

Have you heard about Darren? His dad's been at it again. Tried to steal a suit worth £200 from Marks and Spencers. He might go to jail for five years.

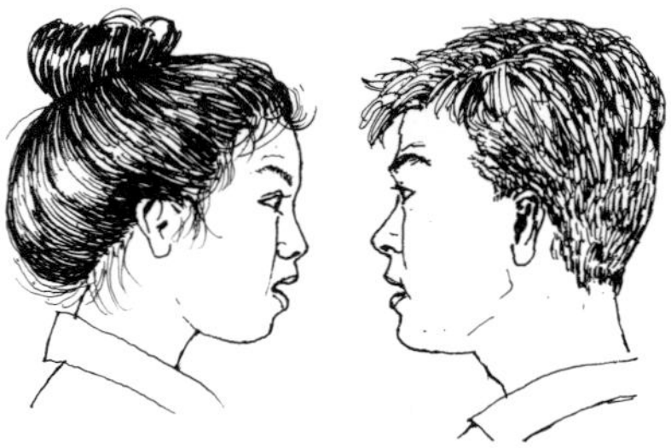

B → C

Heard about Darren Hope? His dad stole £200 from a shop on Christmas Eve. He's going to jail for five years and Darren will have to go into a home.

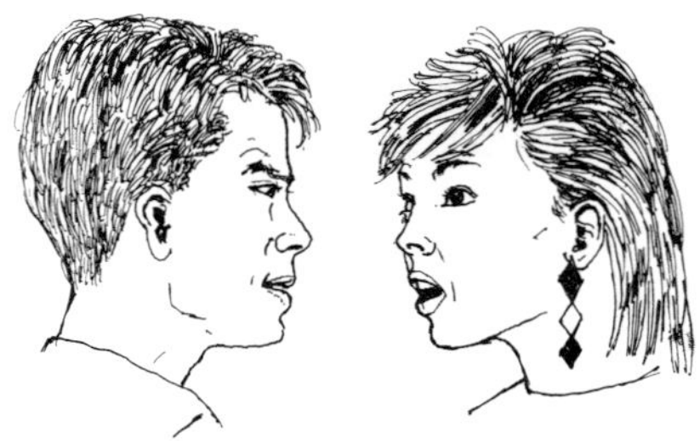

C → D

I know why Darren Hope isn't at school. He's been taken into a home because his dad is in prison for robbing a shop. He stole £2000 and gave half of it to Darren.

D → E

Heard about Hopey? He's been put in a home for helping his dad rob a shop. It was a big supermarket in Manchester. They got away with £10 000. He's too young to go to prison, but his dad will probably get ten years.

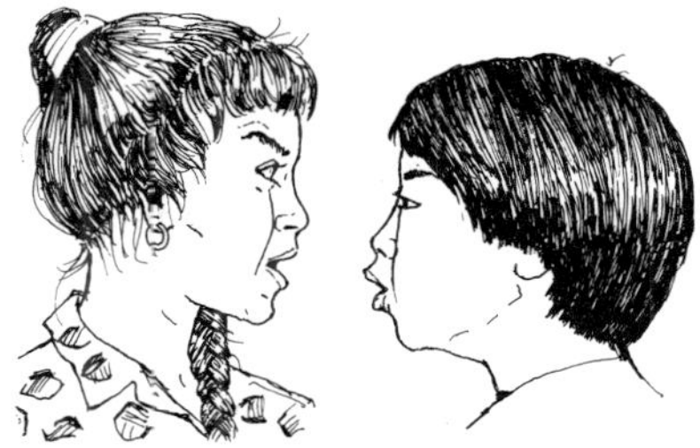

E → F

Have you heard about Hopey? He stole £10 000 from a shop, him and his dad. I always knew he was no good. He's bound to go to prison, and I hope he gets twenty years!

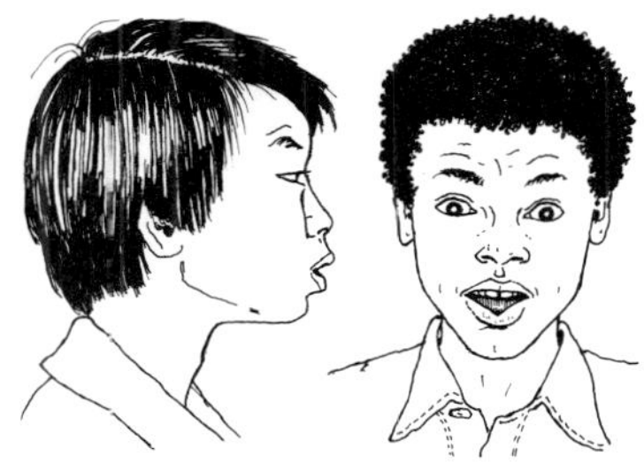

F

What to do

Writing

The original message was changed in two ways:

A The original information was distorted *(distortions)*.
e.g. The jacket became a suit.

B New information was added to it *(additions)*.
e.g. The theft is supposed to have taken place at Marks and Spencers.

1 List three more distortions and three additions.

2 List some of the things that could have caused the message to change as it was passed from one person to another.
e.g. One of the 'tellers' might have disliked Darren Hope.

3 What could you do to make sure that the original message was passed on accurately?

What to do next

Using cartoon faces and speech bubbles, write a chain story like the one given here. Use the list from question 1 above to help you make the changes. The changes should include distortions and additions.

Sex and Death and Father Christmas

When I was 4 years old I learned the truth about sex and death and Father Christmas, in that order, from a girl in our street, called Jennifer.

I was forbidden to play with Jennifer. I wasn't even supposed to talk to her, even though she was the only girl of my age in the street. But because she was strictly 'out of bounds' I soon became her best friend.

Jennifer didn't have special shoes for Sundays. She wore the same shabby dress week in and week out, and it had a sad, sour smell, like our outside loo. She never had pocket money and never went on holiday. She had never been on a train or had a meal in a cafe. But she had something I didn't have, something that drew me to her. She had 'secrets'.

It was Jennifer who told me the truth about sexual intercourse. Her account wasn't that accurate, but it was better than the lies about the 'baby shop' and the 'gooseberry bush' that my embarrassed mother told me.

And when my grandmother died Jennifer painted a very vivid picture of the coffin under the cold, black earth and the worms weaving through the eye holes in the skull, so I knew that Gran wasn't 'watching over me from a cloud' or 'having tea with Jesus'.

It was Jennifer too who banished Father Christmas once and for all, although I never really did believe in him.

What to do

Adults often conceal the truth from young people. For example, if a young person asks, 'Where do babies come from?' their parents might say, 'The stork brings them'.
List as many reasons as you can think of why some parents might not tell the truth in this sort of situation.

What to do next

Oral work in pairs or in small groups

1 When you were young did you believe in things like 'the baby shop'?

2 Is it wrong for adults to tell children babies come from 'the baby shop'?

3 Is there anything that you think can't be discussed openly with young children?

4 At what age do you think young children should be given the facts about:

Sexual intercourse
Drugs
Divorce
Prostitution
Death
Incest
Homosexuality
Adultery
Sexual abuse

What to do next

Role play

Role play a conversation between two parents: one who believes that everything should be discussed openly with young children and one who is strongly opposed to this point of view.

Do you always tell the Truth?

What to do

Give each of these situations a rating from 0 to 10. (A rating of 0 = I find it very easy to tell the truth in this sort of situation. A rating of 10 = I find it very hard to tell the truth in this sort of situation.)

Situations

A If your parents ask you about the boys or girls you go out with.

B If teachers ask you to explain why homework has not been done.

C If you are given an awful present by a very kind relative who has no taste.

D If a friend asks your opinion about their new sweater that you think is vile.

E If a friend asks your opinion about their new girl- or boy-friend.

F If your friend's parents ask you if their daughter or son is taking drugs.

G If the police questioned you about under-aged drinking in you area.

H If you were asked about your 'strengths and weaknesses' in a job interview.

What to do next

1. Compare your ratings with those of other students in your group. In which situations is it most difficult to be truthful? List the things that these situations have in common.
2. Make a list of other situations in which it might be difficult to be truthful. Give each a rating in the same way as you did above.
3. 'It's wrong to tell lies, even white lies. People should always tell the truth.' Write four or five sentences saying if you agree or disagree with this statement. Use information from questions 1 and 2 above to support your argument.

Who's Telling the Truth?

Carl and Tony were having a drink in the pub one night, talking about religion. Carl said, 'Religion is a waste of time. Most people in this country don't believe in a god.' Tony disagreed, saying, 'Don't talk rubbish. The vast majority of people do believe in a god!'
'Prove it,' said Carl.
'Okay, let's both do a survey,' said Tony. 'We'll each ask one hundred people in the street if they believe in a god. That will settle the argument.'

The next night Carl and Tony met at the pub.
'I knew I was right,' said Carl, 'I asked one hundred people and only three said they believed in a god.'
'I don't believe it!' said Tony, 'I asked one hundred people too, but they all said they *did* believe in a god!
'How come?' said Carl.
'Search me,' said Tony.

What to do

1. List some of the reasons why Carl and Tony might have got such different results when they did their survey.
   e.g. Tony might have done his survey on Sunday, near a church.
2. Describe how you would try to get a true answer to the question: 'Do most people in this country believe in a god?'

Bending the Truth

Beryl Briggs' dad is the heavy-weight boxer, Basher Briggs. When Beryl's teachers write her end-of-term report they 'bend the truth' about Beryl to avoid being bent in two by Mr Briggs. Here is part of Beryl's report.

School Report:	
English:	Very good at oral work.
Maths:	She has very quickly learned how to multiply money.
Biology:	Likes experimenting with live specimens.
Physics:	An electrifying pupil.
Chemistry:	Beryl has learned a lot about lab safety this term
Art:	Beryl's artwork is on display all over the school.
History:	She has shown a keen (practical) interest in the Great Fire of London
Geography:	Beryl has worked hard at mapwork and she finds her way to school quite often now.
Games/PE:	She throws the javelin and discus with deadly accuracy!

What to do

Writing
Rewrite Beryl's report, changing the comments so they tell the truth about her awful behaviour. For example:

English:	Beryl never stops talking.
Maths:	She runs a very profitable protection racket.

What kind of person am I?

Who tells you the truth about yourself? Think of six people who know you well. Would they give you an honest answer if you asked them about your strengths and weaknesses?
Write your answers in a table like the one below. Give reasons for your answers.

Person	Honest answer?		Reason
	Yes	No	
Best friend			They would not want to hurt my feelings, or fall out with me.

Councillors not telling the truth

Council in chaos as by-pass plan goes ahead

At a stormy council meeting last night Councillor Terry Mashider said some councillors will 'get rich quick' when the new by-pass around Lanforth is built. The council voted by 11 votes to 3 to go ahead with the controversial by-pass that will take heavy traffic away from the village centre.

Councillor Mashider claims that 6 of the 11 councillors who voted for the scheme 'stand to make a lot of money out of the new road'. He claims they 'did not tell the truth' when they were asked if they had any financial interest in the scheme. When he was asked to give the names of the 6 councillors in question, Mr Mashider made no futher comment.

Leader of the council, Mrs Kate Jones, said bitterly, 'I have challenged him to name names. But he won't. He is scared he will end up in court, charged with libel!' The meeting ended in chaos at 11.15pm.

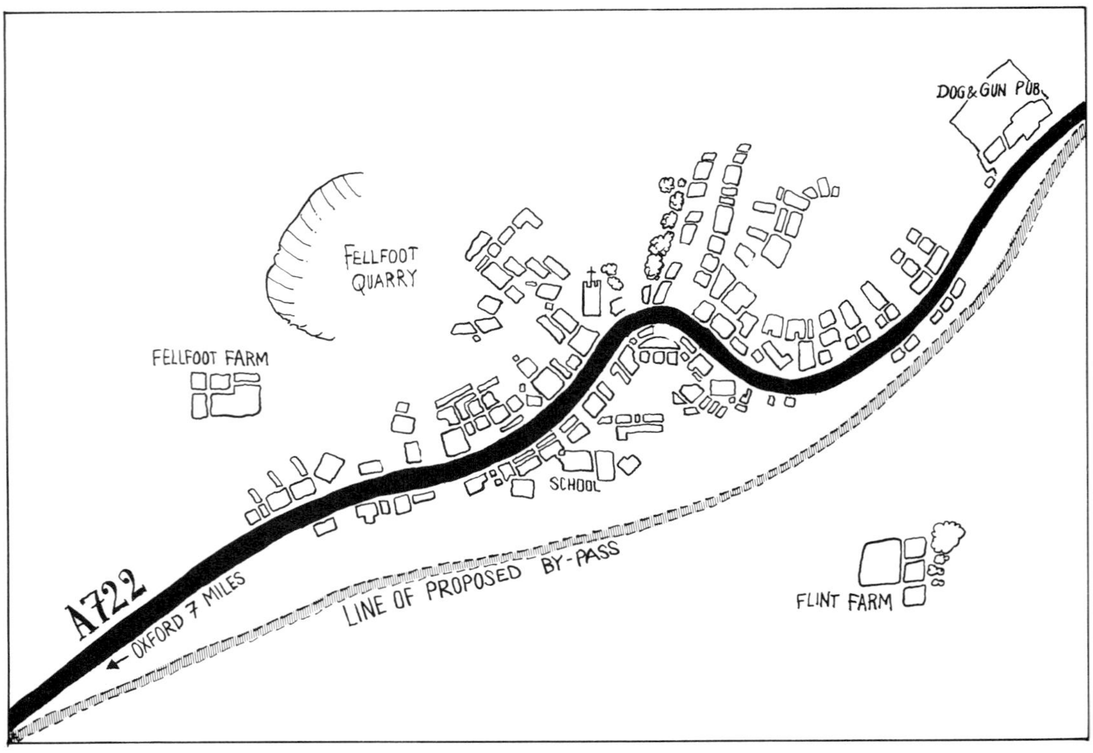

What to do

Here is a list of the 11 councillors who voted for the by-pass scheme.

Councillor	Occupation
1 Mrs Kate Jones	Owns an antique shop in centre of the village
2 Mr Tom Bowker	Retired policeman
3 Mr Julian Barker	Owns the quarry at Fellfoot
4 Mrs Joan Fox	Owns the 'Dog and Gun' pub on the A722
5 Mr Roy Lyon	Retired head teacher
6 Mr Wilf Higson	Owns Flint Farm
7 Mrs Jean Hall	Owns a large building firm in the village
8 Mr John Stanley	Owns a greengrocer's shop in centre of the village
9 Dr John Chippendale	A local GP
10 Mrs Elizabeth Green	Owns a truck company in Oxford
11 Mr Keith Dixon	Owns two guest houses in the village

Study the map opposite and identify any councillors who might make money if the new road scheme goes ahead.

Write your answers like this:

1 Councillor.....may make money from the new road scheme if.....

Pig-in-the-Middle

Trina, Shona and Jeanette are all 15 years old. They have been friends since junior school. Trina and Jeanette are always falling out. When this happens, Shona acts as a 'go-between', like a referee, and tries to get them to make up again. This is what usually happens:

Trina rings Shona:

Trina: I'm sick to death of Jeanette. Do you know what she did today at school? She told that horrible spotty toad in 5G – him with the size 15 feet and sticky-out ears – that I fancy him. I'll break her neck when I see her tomorrow.

Later than evening Shona rings Jeanette:

Shona: Hello Jen. Have you done that Science homework yet?
Jeanette: No, course not. I always do it on the bus coming to school with the other dossers.
Shona: I was hoping you could tell me some of the answers.
Jeanette: You must be joking.
Shona: I rang Trina to see if she'd done it, but she hadn't.
Jeanette: Don't talk to me about Trina Watson!
Shona: Why, have you two had another fight?
Jeanette: She can't take a joke, that's her trouble. She's got no sense of humour.
Shona: I think she's a bit low at the moment.
Jeanette: What do you mean?
Shona: I think her mum's gone off again.
Jeanette: I don't blame her. Imagine having a daughter like Trina Watson. She'd make anyone leave home.
Shona: It must be horrible though, if your mum just goes off, just disappears for weeks at a time.
Jeanette: Suppose so.
Shona: What did you two argue about?

Jeanette: Oh . . . nothing . . . just a stupid joke. Nothing important.

Shona: Why don't you give her a ring, tell her you're sorry?

Jeanette: I might.

Shona: Someone's got to make the first move.

Jeanette: Why does it always have to be me!

Shona: Because you're tougher than Trina.

Jeanette: Don't be stupid. She could flatten me with one hand tied behind her back.

Shona: I don't mean that. I mean you're stronger . . . a stronger person . . . stronger inside.

Jeanette: Big deal. She said she'd break my neck.

Shona: Will you ring her?

Jeanette: I might.

Shona: Will you?

Jeanette I said I might.

What to do

Later that evening Jeanette 'phoned Trina. At first Trina was very aggressive, but Jeanette worked hard to 'close the gap' that her 'joke' had opened between them. Write the conversation between Jeanette and Trina. Set it out like the one above.

Radical Ref's Riot

Last Saturday a mixed football team from Mill Street School played a team from Grant Avenue juniors. It was the last match of the season. The winner of this match would be the local league champions.

The match was to be played at Mill Street School. It was due to start at 10 o'clock. At 10.15 am the Grant Avenue team had not arrived. At 10.30 seven of them arrived with their teacher. The rest of their players were ill in bed, with food poisoning.

The teacher in charge of the Mill Street team said, 'Let's call the game off.'

But the Grant Avenue teacher disagreed. She said, 'No. We want to play. We've been looking forward to this match all season.'

The referee, Ms Jonas, also wanted the match to go ahead. A lot of the players' parents had come along to watch. Ms Jonas didn't want to disappoint them by calling off the match.

The game started at 11 o'clock. At the end of the first half the score was Mill Street 14 – Grant Avenue 0. At half-time Ms Jonas called the two team together. She said, 'This is a very one-sided match. Let's see if we can even things up in the second half.'

First, Ms Jonas made all the right-footed players from Mill Street take off their right boots. Ten minutes into the second half the score was Mill Street 15 – Grant Avenue 4.

Next, Ms Jonas allowed Grant Avenue to have *two* goalkeepers in goal at the same time. Soon the score was Mill Street 15 – Grant Avenue 9.

Then Ms Jonas made Mill Street's ace striker, Mina Hong, wear a blindfold. Five minutes from the end of the match the score was Mill Street 15 – Grant Avenue 14.

Finally, Ms Jonas made the Mill Street team wear ear plugs so they couldn't hear the whistle or each other. The final score was Mill Street 15 – Grant Avenue 15.

At the end of the match there was a riot. The parents wanted to string Ms Jonas up by her boot laces. However, she was saved by the players, who all said it was the best match they had ever played in.

What to do

Oral work in pairs or in small groups

1 What did Ms Jonas do to 'even things up' in the match?

2 What else could she have done to make the match less one-sided?

3 Why do you think the parents reacted as they did?

4 Why do you think the players enjoyed the match so much?

5 How do you think you would have reacted if you had been playing in this match?

6 Do you think Ms Jonas is a good referee?

7 What qualities do you need to be a good referee?

8 Which do you think is the hardest sport to referee?

9 Which do you think is the most dangerous game to referee?

10 Do you think human referees will ever be replaced by machines? Would machine referees have any advantages over humans?

Parents as Referees

A My dad is really mean. When I row with my little sister about what to watch on TV he says, 'I know how to settle this.' He flips a coin. If you win you choose what to watch. I always lose.

B My sister and me are always arguing. My mum never lets me get what I want. She says 'Boys shouldn't bully girls!'

C When I argue with my sister my step-father always takes her side, just because she's five years older than me.

D When I argue with my brother my dad never takes sides. He says, 'If somebody wins then nobody is the winner.' He usually sends us both to bed!

What to do

Oral work in pairs or in small groups

1 Four ways that parents might 'referee' family rows are shown above. Discuss each one in turn and say if you think it is fair or unfair.

2 Who acts as the family row 'referee' in your home? Are they fair?

What to do next

Writing

Working in small groups: Do a survey of students in your school to find out all you can about who referees family rows in their families and how they do it.

You will have to be careful how you frame and ask your survey questions, because some people might be shy about talking about this.

Use the information you gather in your survey to write an article about resolving family rows.

Rent-a-Ref

What to do

Oral work in pairs or in small groups

When two individuals or groups have a disagreement they can't settle themselves, they sometimes ask a third, often neutral, person to help solve the problem.
A person who acts as a neutral judge or referee in this way is called an **arbiter**. Solving disputes this way is called **arbitration**.

1 Do you think the Rent-a-Ref service advertised above is a good idea?

2 What sort of problems do you think Rent-a-Refs would be asked to deal with?

3 Pick one of these problems and say how you might tackle it if you worked for Rent-a-Ref.

4 Do you know any adults who would make good Rent-a-Refs?

Mini-Magistrates

Mill Street School

Mill Street
Milltown
MT1 2AJ

Notice for all 5th year students

Next term we propose to make ten 5th year students Mini-Magistrates.

These students will help me to settle disciplinary problems in school. They wil be expected to act like normal magistrates and take the job seriously.

One of our school governors, Mr Price, used to be a magistrate. He has offered to come into school to train the Mini-Magistrates. If you think you would make a good Mini-Magistrate then get an application form from my office as soon as possible.

Ms R Totton
Head of 5th year

What to do

1 Design an application form that Ms Totton might use to help her select the Mini-Magistrates.

2 Ms Totton wants ten Mini-Magistrates, but over twenty have applied. How should she decide which ten students to choose?

When Ms Totton interviewed some of the students who wanted to be Mini-Magistrates this is what four of them had to say.

A Richard Croll
Form 5A

I think I would make a good mini-magistrate, because other kids trust me. I am very popular in my class and in all the school teams.

B Rachel Frost
Form 5D

You need brains to be a mini-magistrate and because I am in top sets for all my subjects, I think I would be good at it.

C Andrea Lawson
Form 5H

I was always in trouble at school when I was younger so I'm just the sort of person to make a good mini-magistrate. I know what makes the tough kids tick. And they all know me and trust me.

D Colin Clift
Form 5E

My mother is a policewoman so I know all about the law. You need someone who won't be afraid to be tough with these kids, and I'm one of the hardest kids in the school.

What to do next

Writing

1 Write a sentence like this about each of the four students.

A I think Richard Croll would/would not make a good mini-magistrate because .....

2 Choose someone in your class or group that you think would make a good Mini-Magistrate. Write two or three sentences about this person, saying why you think they would be good at it.

Healthy life-styles?

1 Jackie is 19. She lives alone with her six-month-old son in a seventh floor flat. The flat is small, but warm and well ventilated. Jackie doesn't work. She smokes ten cigarettes a day but rarely drinks alcohol. She doesn't know anyone else in the flats. She doesn't go out much.

2 Dave is 16. He lives with his parents and his older sister. He hates any sort of physical activity. He never walks anywhere, he always takes the bus. He doesn't smoke or drink alcohol. At weekends, he stays in bed until 3 o'clock in the afternoon. He reads a lot and watches TV.

3 Jenny is 34. She is married and has two young children. She works part time at a local chip shop. She smokes and drinks quite a lot, and eats fish and chips every day. She goes to the local sports centre twice a week to play badminton. She is a happy-go-lucky person with many friends.

4 Colin is 28. He lives by himself in a comfortable flat. He has a good job as a car mechanic. He hasn't got many friends, because he finds it very difficult to mix with people. He often takes sleeping pills because he has trouble sleeping. He goes for long walks late at night with his dog.

5 Hannah is 87. She lives alone in a cottage in a remote village in Yorkshire. Her eyesight is failing and so is her hearing. She walks about 1 km to the village shop every day by herself, but gets a lift back in the post-bus. She still has a good memory and a sharp sense of humour.

6 Kris is 20. His spine was damaged in a motor-bike accident when he was 18. He can't walk and moves about in a powered wheelchair. He drinks two or three pints of beer a week and smokes a couple of cigars at weekends. He gets depressed sometimes when his parents visit him, because they worry about his future.

What to do

Are the people in the case studies given opposite healthy or unhealthy? Write a sentence like this about each of them:

1 I think Jackie is likely/unlikely to be healthy because .....

What to do next

1 Make a list of all the things that you think are part of a healthy life-style for a young person.

2 Arrange these things in rank order, with the most important one at the top.

3 Compare your list and rankings with those of others in your group. Make a list of the things that were ranked as important by the group as a whole.

4 Use this list to write a paragraph of 6 to 8 sentences describing a healthy life-style for young people.

5 Evaluate your own life-style by completing a table like the one below:

My lifestyle	
Healthy aspects	**Unhealthy aspects**

6 Identify one aspect of your life-style you would like to change. Say why and how you would change it.

What, No Chips?

Shelley was a chipomaniac, a chipoholic, a chip junkie. She was hooked on chips. If she had had her way she would have eaten chips at breakfast, lunch-time and tea-time.

She drove her parents to distraction. Her father would spend hours making a delicious Sunday lunch (avocado pears stuffed with crab, followed by chicken in walnut and cucumber sauce) and all Shelley would say was, 'What, no chips!'

Things came to a head last Christmas when Shelley demanded chips with her roast turkey. Her mother said crossly, 'Starting next week you can eat what you like.'

Shelley couldn't believe her ears.

'But,' said her mother, 'you have to buy and cook the food yourself. We'll give you the money we usually spend feeding you each week. You can spend it however you like. But you won't get any extra money from us, or anything extra to eat. Agreed?' Shelley agreed.

The diary on page 59 shows what Shelley ate for the next seven weeks.

WEEK	COMMENTS
1	Shelley had chips five times a day. She started off making them herself, but soon got tired of that. She became a very familiar face at the local chip shop. The owner started to give her double portions. By the end of the week Shelley's face was very spotty. The money lasted all week.
2	Shelley gave up chips and ate cream cakes and drank diet coke instead. She ran out of money by Tuesday, which is just as well as her jeans were getting tight.
3	Shelley lived exclusively on cheese and pickle sandwiches. She became constipated and the family complained that they could never get into the bathroom. The money lasted all week.
4	Shelley ate nothing but baked beans. This cured the constipation but presented the family with another problem! The money lasted all week.
5	Shelley started to eat out at the local fast-food restaurant. The service was so fast, the restaurant was so hot and noisy that Shelley suffered badly with indigestion. (Also the family took to saying, 'Hello stranger' whenever she appeared at home.) The money ran out on Friday.
6	Shelley bought a pile of frozen TV dinners. But because she didn't defrost them properly she got sick. The money ran out on Wednesday.
7	Shelley decided to do some 'real home cooking' but didn't realize the work and planning this involves. She often sat down to her evening meal (if it hadn't exploded in the microwave) at midnight. The money lasted all week.

Shelley's family were glad when things got back to normal, everyone sitting down together for a delicious meal and Shelley, with a grin, saying, 'What, no chips!'

What to do

Oral work in pairs or in small groups

Answer these questions. Give reasons for your answers.

1 Why did Shelley's mother do what she did?

2 What lessons did Shelley learn during the weeks that she catered for herself?

3 If you were allowed to cater for yourself at home how would this change your diet?

4 If all young people were given a proportion of the family food bill and expected to feed themselves, what effect might this have on young people?

5 What effect would it have on family life?

The Tuck Shop Problem

Teachers Clash Over Tuck Shop Menace

Teachers at a local high school are involved in a bitter argument over their school tuck shop. The shop is run by the school's PE teachers during breaks and lunchtime. It sells sweets, crisps and fizzy drinks.

Health education tutors at the school want the tuck shop to stop selling 'junk food.' They claim the PE department are 'polluting the bodies of the very children they should be trying to make healthy'.

The PE staff make about £4000 a year from the shop. This money is used to buy PE kit and pay for coaches when school teams play away. PE staff claim that without this money 'competition with other schools would be impossible'.

The health education tutors don't want to close the tuck shop. They want to see it selling snacks that are not as 'lethal'. They also want pupils banned from using local chip shops and fast-food restaurants near the school during lunchtime.

The issue will be discussed at a meeting with parents on Thursday.

What to do

Writing

1 Write two or three sentences describing what caused 'the tuck shop problem'.

2 How do you think the problem should be solved?

What to do next

Writing

When the students heard that they might be banned from using local chip shops and snack bars, one of them said:

'I think it's a disgrace. I should be allowed to eat what I like, where I like. It's my body. I can do what I like to it. Chips are bad for you, so what! So is beer and cigarettes. You should see the smoke coming out of the staff room at break-times. And half the teachers go over to the pub at lunch-time. Nobody's telling them what to do. We've got rights, just like anyone else. I think we should go on strike if they try to push us around like this.'

Write a short newspaper report entitled

'Students Strike After Chip Shop Ban'

Use information from the article above to give the background to the strike. Include a comment by a student, a teacher and a chip shop or snack bar owner.